HOW TO PLAY GOLF FOR BEGINNERS

The Essential Guide to Mastering Golf Basics, Techniques, and Etiquette

SAM BROOKS

Contents

Introduction

Golf is one of the world's most popular sports, and it is no surprise why. Stepping onto the greens that seem to stretch out as far as the eye can see while hoping to hit a hole-in-one, the sport challenges and electrifies. Whether you are considering taking up golf for the first time or thinking about dusting off your golfing clubs, we are here to guide you through the process. Think of us as your comprehensive companion, if you will.

Golf is a timeless sport, but it is also so much more than that. Every time you step onto the golf course, you begin a journey leading to perseverance, improved skill, increased patience, and self-discovery. It is a game unlike any other because it challenges the mind and body while captivating the imagination. Let's not forget that the game boosts camaraderie amongst golfers regardless of their age group. It is a sport that brings us together.

We are ready to take you on an adventure where we explore golf basics, from understanding golfing equipment, golf etiquette, rules, and terminology to navigating a golf course's intricacies. Whether you dream of getting a birdie or enjoying more social time with your friends on the greens, our guide will prepare you to make the most of your golfing aspirations.

Congratulations on taking the first step in this fantastic learning experience. Soon, you'll grab your clubs and lace up your shoes with anticipation and confidence. Consider this book your passport to explore the wonderful world of golf.

ONE

Teeing Off with Golfing Equipment

Golfing is considered one of the world's most expensive sports for multiple reasons, including golf memberships, clothes, shoes, and, of course, clubs. Knowing what is necessary to enjoy your first day on the course is ideal because then you get to avoid overspending initially. Instead, you can invest in the necessary equipment and purchase the rest as you evolve in the sport.

Golf Clubs

A golfer is allowed to carry a set of 14 clubs at once. Does that mean you need 14 clubs to begin playing golf? Absolutely not. On the contrary, it is better to start with a small set of clubs and then upgrade to a complete set of clubs once you have mastered the basics. Many golfing shops sell package sets that will give you what you need. Most commonly, these sets will include 2 wedge clubs, a putter, a selection of irons, usually 5, 7, and 9, 2, and a driver.

Is it a good idea to buy second-hand golf clubs?

Everyone knows that golf clubs don't come cheap. However, if you choose them wisely, they are an investment that you can enjoy for years to come. When it comes to buying second-hand clubs, it isn't a bad idea per se. It is vital, however, to keep in mind that avid golfers often have their golf clubs custom-made, and this can lead to unusual specifications that might not suit you.

Therefore, when you are considering a second-hand golf club or set, it is best to see the club or set of clubs in person first before committing. That way, you can tell whether the length, style, and weight are acceptable for you.

A Golf Bag

When you have your first set or half set of clubs, you can hardly step foot onto the golf course without a golfing bag. There is an impressive selection of golfing bags to choose from these days. However, it is essential that you know the pros and cons of every bag type before deciding which is the best for you. Let's take a swing at the four types of golfing bags most commonly spotted on the golf course.

A Stand Bag

As the name suggests, this bag is able to stand while you focus on the game. This bag is very common amongst golfers who prefer to carry their own bags because they come with two straps that allow the golfer to move quickly between rounds.

Pros of a stand bag

• Versatility

• Lightweight

• Comfortable to carry for long distances

• Affordable

Cons of a stand bag

• Limited storage space

A Cart Bag

If you're planning on using a cart while you are on a golf course, it is a good idea to consider getting a cart bag. These bags have been specifically designed to be easily transported by cart. However, if you are not sure whether you'll have access to a cart, or you might not use one every time you are on the golf course, this isn't the ideal bag for you.

Pros of a cart bag

• Multiple storage pockets

• Designed spots for clubs keep your clubs organized

• Easily accessible because of front-facing pockets

• A solid, non-slip base

Cons of a cart bag

• More expensive than other bags

• Heavier and bulkier than other bags

• Not ideal to use without a cart

A Pencil Bag

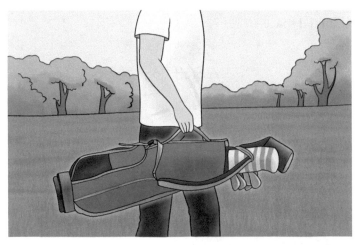

If you have invested in half a set of golf clubs to first test the waters of the golfing world, you might not need to invest in bags that have been designed to hold a full set. Instead, a pencil bag can give you everything you need to hold your smaller selection of clubs. These bags have been designed to comfortably hold up to 7 clubs. These bags are often also referred to as Sunday bags.

Pros of a pencil bag

- Extremely lightweight

- Compact

- Affordable

- Comfortable

Cons of a pencil bag

- It is not practical if you intend to expand your club collection

- Limited space

A Staff Bag

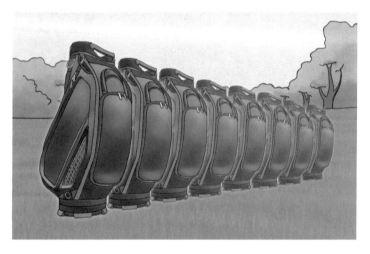

These bags are also known as tour bags. They are generally regarded as the high-range bags that are usually the most expensive on the market. They are designed to store everything that a golfer might need on the course.

Pros of a staff bag

- Impressive storage space

- Excellent organization of clubs, balls, and other items

- Superb durability

Cons of a staff bag

- Priciest of all golf bags

- Heavy and bulky

Which bag is the right bag?

Every golfer has their own needs, so this is a question that every golfer needs to answer. The right bag really depends on your priorities. If you plan on using half a set of golf clubs for some time, you might want to consider getting a pencil bag.

On the other hand, if your golf club offers carts, why not look into getting a cart bag? If you are sure that golfing is a sport that will keep you entertained for years to come, maybe you want to hit a hole-in-one in luxury and invest in a staff bag. While staff bags are most common among professional golfers, stand bags are most preferred by beginner and amateur golfers.

Golf Balls

These days, golfers have endless choices when it comes to golf balls. Just as there is a massive range in the selection of golf balls to choose from, there is a huge range in price. If you are starting out, you might not want to spend up to $50 for a set of new golf balls, as you are already coughing up cash for your golfing bag, clubs, and clothing.

Instead, you can consider buying cheaper alternatives. Many beginner and amateur golfers buy lake balls because they are a fraction of the price and they are in great condition. What is a lake ball, you might ask. Well, as the name suggests, they are balls that have been found in bodies of water. Then, they've been refurbished and inspected. After that, they are sold to golfers.

Are Lake Balls Good Options?

Before lake balls are returned to play, they are inspected by professionals, so golfers who buy them don't need to worry that they might be substandard. However, the pros and cons of lake balls seem to be perfectly weighed up.

On the plus side, lake balls are affordable and environmentally friendly. However, their durability and quality might not be as solid as brand-new balls. Whether lake balls are a good option for you will depend on whether you value affordability and environmental impact more than quality and durability.

TWO

Fitting in on the Course: Dresscode, Rules, and Etiquette

For many years, golf was known as the Gentleman's Game because of its dedication to respect, fair play, and dignity. While these focus points have not changed at all, we are pleased to say that it isn't only enjoyed by the fellas anymore. One of the beauties of golf is the sport's continued commitment to sportsmanship and etiquette.

What to Wear on the Golf Course

Not all clubs have the same views on what players are expected to wear. Some are more stringent, while others are more relaxed. Regardless, it is always beneficial to know the unwritten rules in the golfing world, and understanding the dress code is no exception.

Every golf club has its own membership rules, and the club's dress code will fall under that. The best way to avoid wearing something that won't be allowed is to check out the regulations on the club's website before heading to the greens. It is fair to say that the more prestigious the club is, the stricter they will be on the dress code.

For Men

Polo shirts

A golfer can never go wrong with a polo shirt because it is breathable and looks neat. Most golf courses require a collared shirt, and a polo shirt qualifies. These shirts must be tucked in so the golfer has a neat, polished appearance. You are free to choose whether you want to play in long-sleeved or short-sleeved polo shirts.

Pants

The best pants to invest in are chino pants or golfing trousers. Remember that golf clubs require shirts to be tucked in when choosing a pair of golfing pants.

Shorts

Most golf clubs allow golfers to wear shorts as long as the shorts meet specific requirements. Firstly, they need to have a button-up style and a beltline. Golf shorts should not hang lower than the knee and should fit well. Golfers who show up in baggy shorts that hang between the knee and ankle will probably not be allowed to play. As with the other clothing items, the shorts' color should not be too bold, and the material should be slogan and print-free.

Sweaters, Vests, and Windbreakers

The rule of thumb with these things is that bold colors, prints, and slogans should be avoided.

Shoes

Since golfers walk long distances, wearing the right shoes is very important. Most golfers invest in a good pair of golfing shoes, while others feel comfortable wearing neutral-colored athletic shoes.

For Women

Shirts

There are plenty of great options for women to choose from these days. In most golf clubs, women are allowed to wear sports shirts, V-neck button shirts, turtlenecks, and polo shirts. Some golf clubs will allow female players to play in a blouse without a collar, provided it has sleeves. It is important that women avoid playing in tank tops, t-shirts, and halter tops.

Pants

The best choice for women to play in is khaki golf pants. Neutral-colored slacks are also a viable option. It is best to avoid tights, leggings, and brightly colored or shimmery pants.

Shorts and Skirts

While most golf clubs allow female players to play in shorts and skirts, they might have specific regulations about them. Some golf clubs require skirts to reach the knee, while others are more lenient. However, all golf clubs agree that shorts and skirts can't be unreasonably short.

Shoes

Most women tend to play in neutral-colored, comfortable golfing shoes. However, women are also allowed to play in appropriate athletic shoes and golfing sandals. It is essential to avoid flip-flops, high heels, or overly formal shoes.

For Men and Women

Socks

Most people might not think that socks could ever be an issue, but when you enter the world of golfing, you need to be respectful in all regards, socks included! Neutral-colored, ankle-high socks are the safest choice. However, some clubs will allow knee-high socks if the golfer is wearing shorts.

Headwear

Golfers spend a lot of time outside on the greens, so it isn't surprising that they would want to wear a hat. Most golf clubs are fine with golfers wearing baseball caps as long as they don't have slogans or bright prints. It is vital, however, to keep in mind that hats need to be worn properly, so don't wear a baseball cap backward. Players are allowed to wear bucket hats and visors. Women are allowed to play wearing a sun hat, as long as the color of the sun hat isn't too extreme.

Sunglasses

The margin for error with sunglasses isn't significant. However, it is best to keep to a low-key frame and a good pair of polarized lenses. Oversized, bold-colored frames might be questionable at some golf clubs.

Both men and women should avoid these things:

T-shirts

Most golf clubs require a collared shirt, so wearing a T-shirt isn't ideal.

Jeans

Wearing jeans or denim shorts on the golf course is unacceptable. In fact, it is best to steer away from all denim clothing when you are golfing, including denim jackets or caps.

Cargo or baggy pants

Since golfing is a sport that takes the appearance of players seriously, it isn't ideal to show up in a pair of cargo pants. Also, players who show up with baggy pants or pants that have chains or prints will also not be allowed to play.

Bright shoes or shoes with metal cleats

Most golf clubs have strict regulations regarding shoes with metal cleats because they can damage the greens. If you have your eye on a certain pair of shoes, do yourself a favor and check your golf club's regulations first.

Long socks with bright patterns or prints

Most golf clubs will not allow golfers to play in a pair of socks that draw attention. If you enjoy a pair of bright, themed socks, they are better worn at home.

THREE

The Rules and Regulations of Golf

Golf is a sport that has stood the test of time, and along with its incredible history, a set of rules that have to be followed have developed. Knowing these rules before teeing off will make your golfing experience much more enjoyable.

A stroke-play format is followed

Name: John Smith			Date: 09/04/23								
HOLE	1	2	3	4	5	6	7	8	9	Out	
PAR	5	4	4	4	4	5	3	4	4	37	
SCORE	5	5	5	4	3	5	4	3	4	38	

HOLE	10	11	12	13	14	15	16	17	18	In	Total
PAR	3	4	5	3	4	5	3	4	4	35	72
SCORE	3	4	4	4	5	5	4	3	4	36	74

Handicap: 5
NET: 69

Responsibilities
- Committee
- Player
- Player and maker

Marker's Signature: _____ Player's Signature: _____

Most commonly, golf uses a stroke-play format. This means that the golfer with the least amount of strokes at the end of four rounds is the winner. Usually, each round consists of 18 holes. If there is a tied ranking at the end of the course, a tie-breaker can be completed. This is generally known as a playoff.

A winner will then be determined by allowing the players who are tied to complete extra holes until one takes the lead. Special events, including the Ryder Cup, follow a different format called Matchplay. During this style of golf, players compete over 18 rounds. If a golfer gets the ball in the hole with fewer strikes than their opponent, he or she gets a point.

The winner is the golfer who has the least points after 18 holes. If there's a tie, there will be a hole-by-hole sudden-death playoff to determine the winner. In some competitions, the tied players will play an additional 9 holes.

There are two types of golf courses

Most golf courses have 18 holes. The first 9 holes are generally referred to as the front nine, and the remaining 9 holes are called the back nine. Some golf courses only have nine holes, but they are in the majority.

There is a limit on your clubs

The maximum number of clubs that a golfer can carry on

the course is 14. While golfers are allowed to have less than 14, they aren't allowed to have more.

You need to use one ball for the entire hole

Even if you begin to feel that the ball you've chosen seems unlucky somehow, you are stuck with it. Generally, golfers must complete the hole with the ball they started with. The only exception is if they lose the ball.

You must play the ball as it lies

This rule can be extremely painful for golfers, especially if the ball isn't lying in a good spot. However, the rules are the rules.

The order of play is determined by who lies farthest from the hole

This is generally the rule of thumb when it comes to determining the order of the golfers in the round.

Hit the ball, don't scoop it

Golfers are never allowed to scoop the ball. Only clear hits are allowed.

The green can never be altered

If there is a rock, some leaves, or an acorn in your way, you are welcome to remove it. Loose objects can be removed or moved. However, golfers are not allowed to damage or alter the greens.

Be spatially aware

If you ask any amateur golfer what the most annoying part of golfing with beginners is, they will most likely tell you that beginners tend to stand in their line. This means that you are in the way of that golfer's ball line to the hole. Veteran golfers tend to get very annoyed at this, so take this as a beginner's tip. Try to be alert as to where other players' ball lines might lie.

Respect your caddie

Since golfing is considered a gentleman's game, it is crucial that you respect your caddie and all other players on the greens. Most golf clubs expect golfers to tip caddies, and they will suggest a reasonable amount. If your golf club isn't specific about the tip amount, a good rule of thumb is 20 percent of the cost of the day.

Staying on Top of Etiquette

Since golf is a sport so deeply grounded in tradition and sportsmanship, it is important to be aware of general etiquette on the golf course. By knowing what is considered to be polite and not when taking your first steps on the golf course, you begin your golfing journey on a positive note.

Try to keep the game running at an appropriate pace

It can be frustrating for a different group of golfers if they have to wait for the previous golfers for long periods of time. To avoid this, it is best to be focused and ready to play.

Carry ball mark repair tools and use them

Just as we respect the sport, we should respect the course. Sadly, new players aren't always aware of this, and by neglecting to repair their ball marks, the course isn't in as great a condition as it was when they started.

Don't leave your divots unfilled

Players are generally expected to either fill or replace their divots. For most clubs, either of these options should be fine, but some clubs specify which one they prefer.

Leave the sand bunker as it was

For golfers who take the experience seriously, finding shoe prints on the sand bunker can be very frustrating. That is why raking the sand bunker after use is considered good etiquette.

Don't be a distraction

A big part of golf is challenging yourself. That is why golfers become still and focused before taking that hit. It is considered good etiquette to remain still and out of the way when someone is preparing for a hit. It is also considered good manners to avoid asking golfers questions about the hit they just completed. However, many golfers enjoy discussing their game with their opponents as they go.

Be aware of where the golf cart is allowed to go

If you respect the game and the greens, you should respect the rules of the club. A big part of that is being considerate about where you can drive the golf cart.

Shout 'Fore' if you think someone might get hurt

Being hit by a golf ball can cause some damage, so it is a good idea to warn other players if you think your ball might hit them. A better rule is to avoid hitting the ball if there is another group nearby.

If you are going to the clubhouse between rounds, don't drink excessively

This is an important part of golfing etiquette because drinking too much cannot only irritate other players but also harm our health if we spend too much time in the heat.

If you have music on in your golf cart, keep it down

For most golfers, a big part of the game's enjoyment is the peace and quiet they experience. Some golf clubs allow music to be played in carts, but it is essential that you keep it low enough so that other players aren't affected.

FOUR

Golf Terminology: Understanding the Lingo

As with most sports, golf comes with a wide range of terminology that might be intimidating at first. However, these terms can quickly be learned and understood, and before you know it, you'll be using them, too.

We've put together a list of the twenty most helpful golfing terms that every beginner should know.

Ace

An ace is another name for a hole-in-one. This happens when a golfer sinks the ball with just a single stroke, and it is considered the epitome of golf. Aces most commonly occur on par-3 holes, but it isn't unheard of to happen on a par-4 hole.

Albatross

If a golfer manages to sink the ball with just two hits on a par-5, they have managed an impressive feat. This is referred to as an albatross. Some golfers call it a double-eagle.

Eagle

An eagle also refers to an impressive achievement in golf. This is when a golfer completes a hole two strikes below par, for example, managing to sink the ball with three strikes on a par-5 hole.

Birdie

A birdie is the most common term for positive performance on the golf course. It is when a golfer has completed the hole with one strike less than the par number. For example, if it is a par-4 hole, and the player completes the hole in three strikes.

Par

Par is the recommended amount of strikes that golfers should take on a hole. The par of holes range according to their difficulty level. For example, a par-5 hole will be trickier than a par-3 hole. If a golfer tends to achieve par numbers through the course, the golfer is said to play par golf. On an average golf course, the par number would be 72.

Understanding Golf Handicap

Golf is a sport that players of different abilities can enjoy without anyone needing to sacrifice their game. This is achieved because of handicap, which refers to the average number of shots above par as the round continues. Lower handicaps usually indicate stronger players.

Scratch

If a golfer plays exactly at par or below par, the golfer is referred to as a scratch player.

Bogey

A bogey is basically the opposite of a birdie, meaning that the golfer takes an additional hit above the par number. On a par-3 hole, for example, a golfer who needs 4 hits to complete the hole has played a bogey.

Double and Triple Bogeys

Players who tend to go two hits over the par number have double bogeys. When a player completes the hole with three numbers higher than the par number, he has a triple bogey, often referred to as a trip.

Mulligan

This term mostly refers to friendly play, and you will not see it in a tournament. When golfers are enjoying a relaxing game of golf with friends, they might allow a golfer to retake a shot if the golfer feels unsatisfied with the initial hit.

Caddie

Most people know that caddies help golfers move their clubs around on the course. However, caddies are much more than that. They can offer advice and guidance, especially to new players. Fore-caddies are not expected to carry clubs. Instead, they go ahead of the group so that they can guide them through the game, enhancing every player's game.

Tee Box

The tee box is where you take your first shot of every hole. It is essential that golfers take their first shot within the tee box, or they will be penalized with one shot.

Green

A green is the area where the hole and the flag can be found.

Putt

When golfers use their putters on the green, it is called a putt. Golfers do this to minimize their hits on the green.

Fringe

Greens are generally encircled by areas that have grass that have been cut higher. This area is generally known as the fringe.

Fairways

Between the tee box and the green lies an area of grass that has been mowed very short. This is referred to as a fairway, and the goal of teeing off is for the ball to fall in this area.

Rough

The area with the longest grass around the green and the fairway is called the rough. If a golfer's ball falls here, it can be challenging to get out of it. The ranging lengths of grass add to the excitement and difficulty for golfers.

Bunkers

Golf courses are generally not flat, as that will not be as challenging for golfers to complete rounds. Instead, there are areas that contain sand-filled obstacles. These areas are called bunkers, and there are two types of bunkers. Bunkers that are located close to the greens are called greenside bunkers, while fairway bunkers can be found close to fairways.

Slope

The slope of a golf course refers to the course's difficulty.

Pull and Push

Both of these terms refer to the event where a golfer's ball goes straight on the opposite side of their strongest hand. For example, if a right-handed golfer's ball goes left, it is called a pull. On the other hand, if a left-handed golfer's ball goes right, it is called a push.

FIVE

The Layout of a Golf Course

When avid or professional golfers are asked if they prefer one golf course over the others, they are likely to tell you that they have a favorite. Since there are elements that might make a golf course stand out, it is important to understand the elements that classify the four different types of golf courses.

The Four Types of Golf Courses

Each type of golf course offers its own appeal, so understanding the difference might make it easier to see which one is the best fit for you.

Desert Courses

Large parts of our beautiful planet are dry and arid, but you can still enjoy a round of golf there. These courses found on desert landscapes add exciting elements to the game with elevated terrain, local vegetation, including cacti plants, and rocky backdrops. This is the most common type of golf course in the Middle East.

Parkland Courses

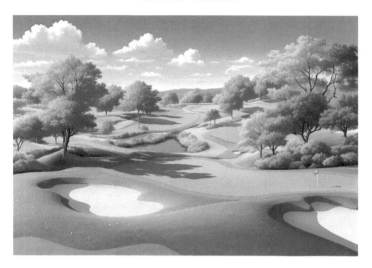

Inland golf courses tend to be green and lush. They are identified by their well-maintained greens and fairways, challenging rough areas, and strategically placed bunkers that increase the course's difficulty level. The most common golf course in the US is the Parkland course.

Links Courses

Initially developed in Scotland, links courses are generally close to the sea, and they are identified by their sandy soil and lack of trees. A common feature of these courses is that they can be quite windy, which adds a challenging factor to the game.

Heathland Courses

Heathland courses offer the perfect middle ground between parkland and links courses. While they tend to be quite sandy, they have more trees and lush greenery than links courses. These are the most popular types of golf courses in the UK.

The Parts of a Golf Course

While each of these types of golf courses offers its own unique elements and features, they all contain the same parts. Therefore, by understanding the parts of a golf course, it will be possible for you to visit any golf course and enjoy a round of golf.

Tee Box

Every hole on a golf course has a tee box. This is the area that indicates where a golfer should stand when teeing off. Some might have multiple tee boxes, and this is to accommodate people of different skill levels. Men and women also have different tee boxes. Here are a few examples of how tees might differ:

Front tees

The purpose of this tee box is to create a short-distance tee for beginners, ladies, or juniors who would like to enjoy a shorter game. These tees are also known as red tees or ladies tees.

White tees

These tees create a moderate distance and are regarded as the tee boxes that offer the most balanced games. They are also called men's tees and they are intended for adult men who have mastered intermediate skills.

Black tees

These tee boxes are designed with professional golfers in mind. These are used at championships and are the longest of all. Black tees are also known as champion tees and their function is to create the most challenging game of all.

Blue tees

These tees are in between the white and the black tees and they are usually used for tournaments. As a result, they are often referred to as tournament tees. They are ideal for advanced golfers who are either playing in a tournament or preparing for one.

Fairways, Greens, and Roughs

All golf courses contain these two areas. However, the level of difficulty, especially in the rough, will vary.

Hazards

Hazards are placed on the course to increase the course's difficulty level. Two types of hazards exist on a golf course: water hazards and bunkers.

Out of Bounds

Not every centimeter of a golf course is meant to be played, and if a player crosses the line that indicates the out-of-bounds area, it results in a penalty shot. If a player has lost his or her ball in the out-of-bounds section, they need to take their following shot from the position they had before they hit the out-of-bounds shot.

The Design Elements of a Golf Course

Every golf course has its own flow, which makes it unique because of its design elements. In fact, no two golf courses are exactly alike.

Course Routing

This term refers to the general layout of the course, including the positioning of the holes and the order in which they should be played.

Strategic Designs

This term refers to the strategically placed areas of a golf course, including hazards, greens, roughs, and fairways. A lot of planning goes into the strategic placement of these things so that golfers have to weigh up the risk that each offers. These elements boost a course's slope since they increase the course's difficulty level.

Elevation Changes

As a golfer progresses through the course, it isn't unnatural to experience elevation changes. In fact, all incredible golf courses offer elevation changes to challenge golfers.

Hole Variety

It is normal for a golf course to have a range of holes, including par-3, par-4, and par-5 holes. Usually, the total par number should be 72 for an 18-hole course.

Doglegs

Not all holes are created equally on the golf course, and doglegs are placed to increase the course's difficulty level. A dogleg is a hole that either leans to the left or the right.

SIX

How to Play the Short Gam

While beginners might assume that the short game refers to the length of time that the game is played, the truth is that it refers to a category of shots made within a short distance from or on the green. Usually, golfers consider shots made within 100 yards (91.5 meters) or less to be in this range. The long game refers to shots made from outside the 100-yard (91.5 meters) distance.

Golfers who have mastered putting with precision and finesse tend to be great at short games, and they can even recover effortlessly if their ball completely passes the green. Short clubs, like wedges, are most commonly used during short games.

Which Shots Belong to the Short Game Category?

There are a surprisingly high number of shots in this category. The main aim of these shots is to cover a short distance accurately so that the golfer doesn't use excessive shots. Let's examine the shots that are used in the short game.

Putt

If the ball is close to the hole, a player might choose their putter to gently guide the ball in. This kind of shot is called a putt.

Off-Green Putt

When a putter is used to get a ball onto the green from outside the green, the shot is called an off-green putt.

Chip

The chip shot is a short-distance shot that is only meant to be used when the ball doesn't need to travel far to the hole but is still on the grass and needs to get onto the green. A golfer will use a club designed to offer a high hit, possibly a wedge, to launch the ball into the air so that it can bounce onto the green.

If a golfer executes the chip shot perfectly and the ball ends up in the hole, it is called a chip-in shot.

The Up-and-Down

This shot involves a two-sequence hit, starting with a chip to get the ball onto the green and ending by using your putter to get the ball successfully into the hole.

Sandy

This also involves a two-sequence shot: the first involves getting the ball onto the green from a bunker using a bunker shot, and the second involves successfully sinking the ball by putting.

Pitch

Often, golfers will use a pitch shot to get the ball closer to the hole. The main feature of this shot is that the ball flies high through the air and lands softly on the green. A pitching wedge is most commonly used to execute this hit, but it isn't the only option.

Pitch and Run

Golfers use this hit to send their ball high into the sky, just to have it land pretty quickly and then roll some distance over the green. Golfers prefer this style if the ground is hard or it is a very windy day.

Bump and Run

This can be seen when the ball takes a quick jump before rolling further on the green. This is a good option when the golfer wants to get the ball onto the green and doesn't foresee any difficulty after the ball lands.

The Bunker Shot

When golfers find themselves in the uncomfortable position of a bunker, they can attempt to get their ball back on the green again by hitting a bunker shot. Golfers refer to powerful bunker shots as explosions or blasts.

The Lop or Flop

If a ball travels a short distance while being very high in the air, it can be called a lop or a flop. Most commonly, golfers use their lop wedge to complete the shot. The aim of the flop or lop is to get the ball on the green without it having enough momentum to roll right off it again.

Lag

Sometimes, a golfer's position might be so awkward that it is more reasonable to aim to get close to the hole than in the hole. A lag shot's primary focus is simply getting the ball closer to the hole.

Which Strategies Will Improve My Short Game?

Golfers who are able to effectively execute all of the shots mentioned above will find the short game enjoyable and less frustrating than those who can't. Therefore, the first thing to do is to practice short-game shots. Short-game success is also reliant on proper grip. Focus on your grip, and ensure that you are using both hands as one unit and maintain pressure consistently.

It is also important that you balance your stance while executing short-game shots. Your feet, shoulders, and hips should be perfectly parallel to the line you hope to achieve.

Practice controlling your distances

Learning to control your distance in golf can be time-consuming and, at times, frustrating, but the payoff is worth it. Therefore, take the time to practice your short-game distances.

Choose wisely

A big part of having a great short game is being able to choose the correct wedge. This is also something that comes with practice, and the more you practice with different wedges, the more you will get a feel for how they function. It is also beneficial to understand the unique functions of every wedge.

Pitching wedges

These wedges can give a golfer more roll and distance.

Sand wedges

A sand wedge is the best choice to get a ball out of a bunker.

Gap wedges

These wedges are best used if a golfer needs something in between a pitching and a sand wedge.

Lob wedges

If a golfer wants a high ball that will have a soft landing, a lob wedge is best.

Practice your pitch shot

The pitch shot is the most useful shot for mastering the navigation of your ball around the green. To achieve an excellent pitch shot, it is vital that you control your swing.

Embrace the benefits of a bounce

Beginners are often intimidated by shots that create a lot of bounce, but these shots can elevate your game greatly. Therefore, don't be afraid to utilize your bounce. Practice shots that make the most of the bounce on the greens.

Practice your chipping

Great chipping skills can get a golfer far on the greens. Therefore, take the time to master effective, controlled, and precise chipping. For successful chipping, much like putting, it is important to keep your stance correct and your grasp firm and concise.

Don't shy away from bunkers

Bunkers tend to be areas of the golf course that beginners would prefer to shy away from. However, practice makes perfect. Therefore, beginners should not avoid bunker play.

Work on perfecting your putting

Improving their putting skills can significantly benefit beginners. It is a good idea to practice putting from various distances and altitudes on the green.

Take the time to examine the green

A big part of golf is learning to be patient. There is no need to rush into a shot. Instead, take the time to look at the green properly. Get into the habit of reading the green before you take the hit. Look at possibly difficult areas, elevated sections, and parts that could lead to unpredictable ball movement.

Enjoy the journey and be proud of your progress

Every golfer has a day on the course that just isn't their day. In fact, most have plenty. The game requires a sense of resilience and a strong mentality. Instead of focusing on what you still can't do, take the time to think about the progress you have made thus far. Golf is not meant to be mastered in a day.

SEVEN

How to Play the Long Game

When a golfer is still far from the green or simply still at the tee box, the player is still busy with the long game. This term refers to shots played from outside 100 yards (91.5 meters) from the green. Golfers who are good at long games are able to effortlessly hit a ball that goes very far and accurately moves toward the green. Different clubs and skills are used to master the long game.

Which Shots Belong to the Long Game Category?

There are fewer shots for the long game. By understanding the shots used in the long game, it makes it easier to master your long game.

Drive

This term refers to the shot taken from the tee box. Most commonly, golfers execute this shot using their drivers. However, golfers are not required to use a driver to make the drive shot. Players have to hit the ball within the tee box, or they will receive a one-shot penalty.

Three-Quarter Shot

It isn't always ideal for golfers to use 100% of their backswing, or they risk losing their ball or going past the green completely. When a golfer chooses to use only 75% of their backswing, the shot is called a three-quarter shot.

Lay Up

Sometimes, a golf course presents the golfer with possible problematic features, including trees, hazards, or unusual elevations. To avoid getting the ball in an uncomfortable position, the golfer might choose to execute the lay-up shot, a short-distance shot meant to get the ball on the fairway. Since this shot isn't meant to travel long distances, most golfers will choose a wedge to execute it.

The Knockdown or Punch Shot

Sometimes, golfers can't send their ball high into the air. In this case, they will choose to launch a long-distance ball that travels lower to the ground. These shots are called knockdowns or punches.

Approach

This term refers to a shot taken with the goal of getting it onto the green. When a golfer chooses to take an approach shot, it will depend on the difficulty of the hole. For example, on a par-5 hole, a golfer might decide to try to get the ball onto the green by the third shot, making the third shot the approach shot. If a golfer wants to achieve a high approaching shot, it is best to choose an iron 3 to 9. It is not uncommon for golfers to use their wedges for their approach shots. It really just depends on the golfer's preference and goal.

The Blind Shot

As the name would suggest, this shot is taken when the golfer can't see what lies ahead. Most commonly, this happens when a golfer's ball is behind a large tree. The golfer uses a blind shot and hopes for the best.

Which Strategies Will Improve my Long Game?

As with every part of golf, mastering your long game takes time, commitment, and patience. There are ways that you can master your long game more effectively.

Practice your accuracy

Since the long game involves long distances, accuracy can make a big difference. It is essential to take the time to get familiar with different clubs and shots. With effort and determination, you will see progress in your accuracy.

Improve your distance

As you become more familiar with the long game shots and clubs, you will see an improvement in your distances too.

Decreased scores

One of the first things you should notice as your accuracy and your distance improve is decreased scores. However, this doesn't happen on the first day of teeing off. Golf is a commitment, and it is important to enjoy the journey.

Choose wisely

Similarly to the short game, choosing the correct club is essential to enjoying a great long game. It is important to keep in mind which clubs offer which unique features.

Driver

This club is most commonly used to tee off. It is the longest club in any golfer's set of clubs, and it has specifically been designed to cover long distances.

Woods

These are also used for long-distance hits. Generally, the lower the number of wood, the further the ball will go.

Long Irons

These clubs are great if you want to cover a great distance while not sacrificing your control over the ball.

Hybrids

These clubs are a combination of a wood and an iron club. They are ideal for long-distance shots from the fairway or rough.

Utility

These clubs are great for golfers who have yet to master their long irons. They are suitable for tee-offs and long-distance hits from the fairway.

Know where you're at

Most beginners feel frustrated when they overestimate their abilities. However, beginners who keep their skill level in mind when choosing the right clubs improve faster.

Examine your distances

It isn't ideal for golfers to be impatient, and even more so for beginners. Instead, take the time to estimate the distance that you want to achieve.

Keep the weather in mind

If the weather is perfect, you probably won't feel much interference, but it is a different story on a windy day. The wind can greatly affect gameplay, so it is essential that golfers keep the wind in mind before choosing long game shots. Instead of choosing a high-ball shot on a windy day, stick to the knockout shot that will keep your ball low to the ground.

Maximize your power setup

The way you prepare for your hit makes a lot of difference in golf. When you are ready to hit the ball, take a second to evaluate your stance, your hands, and your grip on the club.

Use your left arm to create lag

When you do a backswing, there is an angle between your left arm and your club. This is known as lag. It is best to create lag when you are playing a long game. The easiest way to create sufficient lag is to focus on keeping your wrists steady and firm as you swing back.

Focus on the follow-through

After your club has made an impact with the ball, it's not over yet. You still need to follow through. Do this by making sure that your weight has been shifted to the foot in the front. By now, your arms should be extended and facing your target line.

Increase your clubhead speed through impact

In order to hit those high, stretching hits, you have to accelerate through your impact.

EIGHT

Managing Expectations and Understanding the Psychology of Golf

The fact that golf challenges players physically, mentally, and psychologically is a blessing and a curse. Many beginners make the mistake of having unrealistic expectations. In fact, countless beginners have given up after a few days because they felt that they weren't showing any progress, which led them to think that golfing was simply not for them. That is a pity because it is a gratifying sport, but like most things that are great in life, it requires some sweat and tears to master the game.

Tips for Managing Your Expectations

Let's take a look at some of the best tips and tricks to keep in mind when managing your expectations.

Don't compare yourself to others

A massive part of golf is its focus on self-improvement. It is not a competition or a racc to get to master level first.

Instead, you are focusing on your own improvement. Many beginners make the mistake of comparing themselves to golfers they see on the TV or on the golf course.

Most of those players have been playing for years, so it is not a fair comparison to make. In addition to this, the conditions that players on the TV are playing in might differ from yours. It is simply best to keep your eye on the prize: improving your own golfing skills.

If you are practicing, don't focus too much on the score

Beginners can always benefit from practice. In fact, practice never hurts any golfer, regardless of their skill level. However, if you have decided to spend a morning on the course practicing your putting, for example, focusing on the number of hits you need to make it to the hole might be more demotivating than anything else. The bottom line is if you are practicing, you are doing what you can to improve, and that is what your goal should be.

Don't shy away from the opportunity to practice your skills

Often, beginners might feel insecure when it comes to playing with other golfers. However, everyone starts somewhere If you get invited to join other golfers in a friendly game, why not join them? Most golfers are very supportive because they know they are also beginners.

Set small achievable goals

If you've just begun playing golf, making it your goal to win the club championships in a month is not a very realistic goal. An unreasonable goal can do much more damage than good. Small, realistic goals, on the other hand, can boost a beginner's confidence and inspire the player even more. What would be a reasonable goal, you might ask. Well, what about making your first goal to get the ball airborne from the first tee?

As you improve, you can adjust your goals, moving onto a goal like aiming to make par, for example. If there is an area that you find particularly challenging, why not focus on that for a week or two? If bunkers frustrate you, get over the frustration by practicing your bunker shots. When you achieve your goals, take the time to celebrate this small but relevant victory.

Don't get too wrapped up in the details

The main focus of a beginner should be to get out and play. If you are too focused on technical details, you might find that you don't enjoy the game as much. Instead, enjoy playing freely and keep your goal to improve the game, not to be technical about everything.

Don't rush yourself

This refers to rushing yourself before you take a swing and in regards to your goals. Golfing is more than just a sport, it is an experience that is meant to boost the body and mind. If you rush yourself, you take that wonderful experience away from yourself. If you are generally an impatient person, remind yourself to slow down.

Don't shift blame

Golf is a gentleman's game, and gentlemen don't shift the blame. If you are having a bad day, it is not the clubs that didn't perform well or someone who was also on the course. Accepting that you are going to have good days and bad days is an important part of mastering the sport.

Take the time to enjoy it

A day spent on the course is a good day, even when the game isn't going your way. Remember to enjoy the experience.

NINE

Understanding the Psychology of Golf

Golfers will agree that golf is so much more than the physical act of hitting a few balls with a set of clubs. It is also much more than meeting up with other golfers at the clubhouse after the game. The game requires patience, persistence, and a strong mentality. This explains why some golfers might have a horrible day followed by a great day the next. It all has to do with golf psychology. Our minds are powerful tools that can easily affect our performance.

What should I focus on to boost my mentality in golf?

There are a few things that affect our mental status every day. If you keep these things in mind, you can boost your mental toughness, even on days when the game isn't going your way.

Confidence

If you are not feeling confident, the game will likely not go your way. This is because of your mind's ability to affect your performance. If you are preparing yourself mentally to have a disastrous game, the outcome will most likely not look great. It is tricky, though, because we all have days when we just don't feel very confident. Having a bad day on the course while we are not feeling confident will not do our confidence any favors. Is there a way to stay confident even on the days that you might not feel it fully? Absolutely! There are three effective ways to keep your confidence up.

✔ Visualization of the positive outcomes you hope to see

✔ Setting reasonable goals

✔ Keeping your self-talk positive

Concentration

Golf is a precision sport that requires concentration, but ironically, a golf course is filled with objects that can easily distract a beginner. Birds chirp in the trees, and leaves rustle in the breeze. Golf carts spin the distance, and other golfers enjoy chatting on the course. How can you keep concentrating when there are so many distractions?

✔ Create a routine to keep you focused before you take a swing and stick to it

✔ If the previous shot wasn't great, don't dwell on it. Instead, focus on the moment you're in now.

✔ Use mindfulness techniques, including visualization and deep breathing

Staying in control of your emotions

Most golfers know that golf can be a wild rollercoaster ride that explores a wide range of emotions. However, by mastering emotional control, a golfer will enjoy increased mental toughness on the course. Here are three techniques that can boost your emotional control.

✔ Accept the game and your performance

✔ Keep your mind on your progress, not your results

✔ Learn how to navigate your emotional awareness

Practicing resilience

There are many things that can go wrong in a game of golf, but how a golfer bounces back from these setbacks makes all the difference. If you tend to feel like you want to give up the minute your tee-off doesn't go as well as you hoped, you should consider focusing on resilience. Three techniques can boost your resilience.

✔ Stop dwelling on errors of the past

✔ Keep the 'it's-a-game' perspective

✔ Focus on having a growth mindset

Visualization

The saying goes, "If you can see it, you can achieve it." Being able to picture the results you want in your mind's eye can significantly boost your performance and mentality in golf. Here are three ways that you can boost your visualization while on the course.

✔ Include sensory details when you are picturing your ideal outcome

✔ Be visual about problem-solving on the course

✔ Create a mentally positive routine and stick to it

Additional techniques to unlock your full potential on the golf course

Golfers who understand that golf requires a combination of strong, healthy golf psychology and skill development show more remarkable progress and find the game much more enjoyable. These three tips are essential in boosting your mental state when you think of golf.

Golf needs to be enjoyed in a positive environment.

The people who play with you are a part of that. If you are not feeling uplifted by those you share the excellent game with, you might need to find new players to hang out with.

Don't shy away from improvement plans

If you get worked up on the course, take time before you decide on what you would like to improve first. It is easy to feel overwhelmed if you've had a bad day, and then it might be hard to pinpoint weaknesses that require your focus.

Communicate with others

One of the many good things about golf is that everyone has a bad day on the golf course. There isn't a golfer out there who has never felt disappointed and frustrated on the course. By communicating about the journey with others, you will not feel like you are the only one struggling with golf. Along with boosting your mental health, other golfers are usually also very eager to share tips on what helped them when they were beginners.

TEN

Getting Out of Trouble Fast

Most golfers know the feeling of finding themselves in an unideal position that they just don't know how they would recover from. Luckily, there are five shots that are guaranteed to get you out of any sticky situation, from being stranded between the trees to just being grossly out of position.

By knowing these five shots and how to execute them effectively, there won't be a scenario on the golf course that will have you scratching your head. It is essential to keep in mind, however, that similar to all shots in golf, these shots need to be practiced before they can be perfected.

What Are the Five Shots That Can Get You Out of Trouble?

Here are the shots you need to keep up your sleeve when you get in trouble out on the course.

The Right-Handed Only Shot

Sometimes, the placement of the ball makes it difficult for the golfer to stand in the traditional way. An excellent example of this will be if your ball is on the edge of a bunker. A golfer can get out of this awkward position by standing with their back to the target line. While holding the club with the right hand only, the golfer can gently chip the ball to move it away from the danger zone.

The Left-Hander Shot

This shot involves using a 9 iron. The golfer should flip the club round so that the golfer hits it left-handed with his or her toe facing down.

The Hover Shot

Beginners can find it very tricky to navigate the ball on the rough. This is because the ball tends to lie relatively high. The best way to deal with this is to use a tall driver tee and a 6-iron.

The Belly Wedge

This shot can be achieved by using a sand wedge on an area with longer, thick grass. By choosing this club and using it as a putter, you will create the ball that should move over the grass at a speed similar to a putt.

The Low Punch

This shot is best for distances of 100 yards (91.5 meters) that offer some trees so that the ball needs to remain low to the ground. Using a 5-iron is perfect for this shot.

Course Management

Course management is a very important part of golf because it involves using a player's strengths to get the ball into the hole with the fewest hits. Successful course management also helps golfers assess their performance, track their strokes, and control their swings and putts.

What are good strategies for course management?

Here are some of the best strategies for golf course management.

Understand your strengths and the stats of the course

Golfers who clearly understand what they are good at and what they're not good at tend to enjoy the game much more. In addition, players who take the time to observe the course and try to establish the layout and distances have more success, too.

Lay-Ups aren't negative

Beginners tend to think that it is more important to get the long shots so that they can minimize their par. However, if there are hazards or features on the course that could make your next hit problematic, there is nothing wrong with maximizing your lay-up.

Don't experiment with new shots if you have your heart on winning

If you feel like today you really need a win to keep your heart in the game, stick to the shots that you have been practicing. If you are already struggling with your mentality on a tough golf day, choosing shots that you have never practiced might make you feel deflated and unmotivated.

Instead of aiming for the flag, aim for the middle green

This is a very valuable tip for beginners because they tend to keep their eye only on the flag. However, by making it your goal to land the ball on the green, your course management becomes much more accurate and stress-free.

Enjoy the positive days

Most golfers know the thrill of having a positive streak day on the course. When this happens, enjoy it because golf can be unpredictable. By utilizing a positive streak, you have the opportunity to boost your scores and minimize the odds of hitting a bad shot.

Don't bring too few clubs

By not bringing enough clubs, a golfer really limits his or her options. Therefore, as long as you have no more than 14 clubs with you, bring as many as you can manage. By doing this, you also give yourself more opportunities to practice using different clubs.

Fortune favors the bold

Sometimes, an excellent outcome comes with some risks. If you see the odds might be in your favor, go for it. However, remind yourself to be aware of your emotional control so that you don't take it too badly if it doesn't work out as you might have hoped.

Sometimes, it's better to play it safe

Many golfers will agree that golfing shouldn't be played aggressively and if you aren't sure about the outcome, it is fine to stay safe. Whether you are the kind of golfer who wants to take the risk or play it safe, is up to you.

Don't seek out the problematic areas

If you are a beginner, stick to the more manageable parts of the course. By being aware of the areas that should be avoided, you give yourself greater odds of an enjoyable game that will have you feeling confident and calm.

See your mistakes as learning opportunities

Pro-golfers will agree that golfers learn more from their mistakes than from anything else in golf. Therefore, if you make a mistake, don't beat yourself up about it. Instead, take what you can from it and become a better golfer because of it.

Keep your recovery shots reasonable

If you are in a difficult position, it is better to keep your recovery shot sensible. By going overboard with bravado, you might make a tricky situation even more difficult to recover from.

ELEVEN

Conclusion

Alice Cooper famously said, "Mistakes are part of the game. It's how well you recover from them; that's the mark of a great player." Taking up golf is taking the first step into a journey of self-improvement, improved health, and increased mental health.

While we have reached the end of this book, this is just the beginning of your exciting golf adventure. Golf is a sport that isn't limited by age or the skills of the player. Instead, it is a sport that offers endless opportunities for players to connect with others, experience self-growth, and enjoy the outdoors.

Remember that every golfer was a beginner once. Every round you spend on the golf course is an opportunity to learn and improve, so embrace it. Every bogey and birdie is part of your unique golfing adventure, one that will be filled with unforgettable moments, setbacks, and triumphs.

Your most outstanding rounds are yet to come, so grab your clubs and head to the golf course.

Made in United States
Troutdale, OR
10/25/2024

24127206R00056